The Dear Queen Journey:
A Path To Self-Love

Sylvester McNutt III

CONNECT WITH MY SOCIAL MEDIA
WEBSITES LISTED BELOW:

WWW.SYLVESTERMCNUTT.COM

WWW.FACEBOOK.COM/SYLVESTERMCNUTTIII

WWW.TWITTER.COM/SYLVESTERMCNUTT

WWW.INSTAGRAM.COM/SYLVESTERMCNUTT

WELCOME TO

THE DEAR QUEEN JOURNEY: A PATH TO SELF LOVE

The spark for writing was the desire to understand my own feelings and thoughts, because I didn't feel comfortable sharing them in my environment as a child. I started writing a journal at the young age of twelve to compensate for my lack of trust in my ability to feel safe expressing my words. This was a very turbulent time for me, as I was entering puberty, and the abyss of life that became my parents' breakup devoured our family whole and split us into separate sectors of minimized love.

The change of growing from a boy to a teenager, and from a family to a broken mirror of portraits of what used to resemble a family, became the original reason that I constructed lines of pain, joy, and passion every single day of my life in my journey journals. Writing became my escape and safe haven from the world that corrupted my naïve view of life. As I was thrust into fight after fight, failure after failure, and relationship loss after loss, eventually enough became enough.

I started writing this specific project because I grew frustrated with "loving" and losing it over and over—not just in the relationship aspect, but in general, as the relationships with my father and mother both fizzled out via the adversity of distance, difference, and dissonance. The tension submerged my conscience in anger and violence, and self-love was absent from my temple. I knew that I was on a crash course for suicide or homicide if I didn't change my behavior, mind-set, and structure. However, suicide was the only way I could actually live, so I systematically killed myself day by day. I started a journey called the Identity Route. This was the day that I understood I didn't know anything, I didn't love myself, and I could not continue carrying the mask of self-hate, as it perpetuated insecurity, fear, and doubt. After concluding a year of my Identity Route (self-awareness), I then started *The Dear Queen Journey* (self-love). I felt like it was necessary for me to objectively break down the answer to the question, "Who am I?" Understanding who you are is something that most people never try to do, simply because the task is too overwhelming. *The Dear Queen Journey* is not about finding a queen in the wife aspect, and from the female perspective, it is not about finding a man; this journey is about finding yourself. Throughout history, a queen has always been the symbol of love and success when it comes to love.

The queen is the most powerful piece on the chessboard; the queen is the reason countries fight and the epitome of what we aspire to be. Women want to be respected and cherished in the same way a queen would be, and no man wants a peasant woman—he wants a queen. So *The Dear Queen Journey* is our exploration through transparency, objectiveness, and awareness as we grow and learn what self-love is and how we can elevate ourselves in order to deliver love, receive love, and be loved every single day.

If you isolate your heart, you cannot get upset when there is no one present to warm it. The healing, forgiveness, and moving-forward process starts with closure. My offer for said closure is self-love.

- Sylvester McNutt

The Dear Queen Journey,

I'm highly intoxicated with the pleasure of your presence. One day I will discover your warm body next to mine. We will both shake as an eruption from the equator shifts our balance off an even keel. You feel the rotational pull of the earth navigate around you with every step that we take away from each other's epicenter of love. I want you to take a ride, a ride with no equivalence or comparison. I plan to give you a feeling so intertwined with your perception of nirvana that you coil under my spell of passion and devotion.

This book exists because my desire is to enter, understand, and appreciate the feeling of practicing self-love. This book is about love; it's about the pain and the journey. It's all about coming from nothing and making it something; they refer to it as "alchemy," turning nothing into something—a truly magical process. I believe that our culture deserves love. It deserves a better appreciation of the true essence of love. Let's be frank: we are blind and naïve to the true potential of love because we have not studied it enough. We have not studied our own core enough to understand our processes and inner workings.

How do we expect love to permeate our souls if we do not train ourselves to allow the purity of the emotion to dominate our baseline of logic? How are we supposed to love other people if we never consistently practice loving ourselves? If love is eternal, then why don't we focus on the internal aspect of it? Love is something intrinsic, so why do we expect anything external to solidify and validate the substance of something that is purely internal?
- Sylvester McNutt

Our logic is flawed because we introduce our representatives to people, and in some situations, we show only our representatives to people instead of revealing our true self. It's time to kill your representative so you can represent you in all interactions. We have expectations of people instead of acceptance for them. The key is to accept ourselves as we are. The key to love is acceptance. This journey is about finding ways to accept our own images and selves as we are and as we will be. It's not about searching for or finding acceptance; it's literally about the *is*-ness of accepting acceptance.
- Sylvester McNutt

The transparency, the vulnerability, and the uniqueness of who you are should never be marginalized by anyone else's insecurity, fear, or weakness.

- Sylvester McNutt

The capabilities that you have as a human literally have no maximum potential. You're an endless being, but you have to believe that there are no barriers. We use the word "love," but love literally has no walls or barriers. As we start *The Dear Queen Journey*, I challenge you. I challenge you to let go of the pain, thoughts, and images of the past. I challenge you to accept that this book will change your mind-set and open you up. You're terrified to completely open yourself up and remain vulnerable, as you feel that poison will drip into your wounds. The fear you have will vanish, the walls you have will be the walls that become broken, and the rubble will be used to build your bridge to self-love. Our stories are unique and united because we have the same desire. We desire to have love and to belong. Trust me: we are the new kings and new queens of the new culture. This is our culture to shift. We will win by shifting our mind-sets, shifting our abilities, and accepting a new lease on life.

Loving Yourself

Loving yourself is the most important task we should focus on. Our society does not allow us to permeate the truths of our own identities. I believe that each person should practice forms of self-love. There's nothing like finding out who you are, appreciating your own life for what it is, and being able to confidently exist as the highest version of yourself.

Self-love is about developing behaviors that nourish you; you deserve to receive the light and peace you desire. Self-love is about finding fitness activities that suit your age, body type and desire. Self-love will always be an action, and is less of a feeling.

If you feel lost or unsure of your direction, do not over analyze. Accept everything, as it is; grow naturally without force. Self-love is the ultimate gift you can give yourself.

This society, culture, and period of technology teach us that we have to compare ourselves to others. They teach us that we are not acceptable and lovable as we are. I call bullshit; it wasn't until I actually "tried" to love myself that I discovered I actually did.

The life before self-love practice was one that had lots of absent love. Now there's so much consistent love in my life that complaints or even an acknowledgement of anything less would simply be egregious. The best way to start loving yourself is to release your emotional connection to people, places and instances in your past that prohibit you from moving forward. I found it easier to love myself once I started practicing better eating habits, listening to cleaner music and the most important behavior was letting go of the consentient need to judge myself.

Dear Queen: Clark First

I've cried out for, craved, and done everything to attract your attention. It's as if my effort has pushed you away. It's that feeling of "no matter what you do, nothing is good enough." It's as if I'm walking on eggshells. As godly, powerful, and creative as you are, there's still a gap. There's that gap of closeness that is necessary to close; I call it the "Great Wall."

You're so damaged from your past, so set on protecting your morals, values, and yourself, that you have given nothing; you've forgotten the universal rule of life: "To gain, you must sacrifice." It's an equivalent exchange, my dear. Even if you feel that the reciprocation may not be equal within human behavior paradigms, please push your mind to understand a level of understanding that is not present—"To gain, you must sacrifice."

It's universal law. Example—if I want to pass this test, I must study. Queen, in order for me to succeed with my test, I have to give up time to focus. Queen, in order for you to be loved, you have to give up the Great Wall; you have to give up the anger from the past. You need to undergo a purging of your soul and you must activate a forgiveness channel to release all the toxic poisons that haunt you daily.

Queen, I have scars that penetrate my skin like salt on an open wound. I've shed tears the same as you. I've contemplated my purpose and had to answer questions the same as you. I ask you to understand—you and I are both *humans*. These struggles do not define us; they have simply been a part of the agile life we are accustomed to. It does not make us weak because we had a moment of weakness; it just makes us experienced. I believe you want Superman, but you haven't even seen Clark.

I believe that if you want someone to protect your inner and outer with all of his power, you should rectify your shell of the past. I think some self-healing is in order. Why don't we self-heal together? Let's meditate, pray, and allow thought to cycle through your emotions. Understand that we have the power to connect souls and shift the universe. The rest is up to you. Do you accept the mission of seeing the Clark in me and yourself first? Before we can activate our superpowers, we have to understand that we are just basic creatures at the core. Is this something you're ready to accept? Understand that you are worthy. Understand that you deserve this. Understand that no superpowers can be activated until we accept our average roles every single day when we wake up.

March 27 - Mirrors

Mirrors, mirrors
They're supposed to show me what I am
In a bubble of confusion
Look around
She loves me, she loves me not
She loves my money
I see a lack of trust
My life lacks everything
Most of all, a lack of love!
All I want to do
Is make it right
With one
Tired of the pain and heartbreak I cause
It might be karma
I'm breaking down walls
No vision, no feelings
She writes me a letter
Just a coldhearted chamber
Remember my name
I'll be gone in September
Remember my hair, her long brown hair
Remember the nights I was playing in it
Laying in it
She's my favorite
I'm a raven, but she's more like an eagle
Flew away with my heart
Will she ever come back?
Or is she lost to the people?

May 17th - Dirty Eyes

If eyes really reveal the soul,
I can't read her look.
I'm not sure if she's confused at her life up to this
point,
Or if she's telling me to run.
Maybe I can see the pain perfectly clear,
Reflecting back at me as if I'm projecting it onto her.
She understands my pain because of her own.
Her eyes just tell me she's tired of being alone.
She tells me the attention she gets bothers her,
But she settles for now.
She's not concerned with being popular.
Her eyes are curious to know if I have what it takes.
But she knows I'm too weak, so she keeps looking
past me.

Approval

There's this idea of "approval." I suppose it's acceptable if we're making decisions together, such as in an intimate relationship. However, this approval and the need for it from others that I observe can cripple people. I feel like people allow fear and mystery to revolve around particular ideas or behaviors until there's that said approval level. I offer this statement of understanding that I've acquired:

"You don't need approval to improve yourself." Our minds were engineered to remain curious and to keep learning. If you're not exploring new versions of your own mind, then you're dying. Allow this said approval seeking to die and allow your curiosity to live; it's the only way to abolish the fear and live without approval. Lastly, remember that nobody validates you besides your own self.

Dear Queen: The Moment

There is a desire that burns inside of me to be with you in ways I've never imagined. Meeting you has changed my life like the winter equinox. You're warm when I'm inside of you, like a pizza box. You're close, so close I can feel the goose bumps on your back rise as I run my tongue down your thighs. I can feel your spine shiver and vibrate as I race my tongue down your fireplace.

Slow, soft kissing—kissing so real, so passionate, I can feel the smooth ridges of your lips against mine. My love, you are Goddess, and in the midst of this session, your scent is so intoxicating, it's addicting. My favorite part is grabbing your neck after I warm you up, not to hurt you but to let you know I'm in control. This gesture you reciprocate by locking eyes and pushing my hips closer to your spot, letting me know you're in control. Chest to chest now, the sweat sears together to make one layer of flesh. I feel your nails as they dig into my back muscles. Your head slowly starts to rotate back, like in road-trip drowsiness. The R&B music in the background becomes the theme music for this scene. Then, as "the moment" happens, millions of signals go off in your brain. You're erupting mentally as your heartbeat rises to a beat-per-minute ratio that is unsafe—this is the moment. **Soak Up The Moment** The idea of me spending time with you resonates so deeply within my mind. I want to soak up these moments, because in my past I've learned that love can be fleeting. There must be a way, Queen, that we can let love reproduce itself over and over again. I have an idea: What if, my love, we understand that we'll need space? What if, as a man, I try to be more affectionate? What if, as a woman, you try to respect me more? What if we both agree to speak to each other with love? No, we don't have to agree, but could we disagree without war? My goddess, this world is nothing without you. Let's combine our powers for an everlasting connection that is rooted in love, how does that sound to you? Good morning, my love. It's been a while since I wrote you. Honestly, the turmoil of my life has been putting pressure on my soul. It's released when I see pictures of you. It's like your face takes my mind to a safe haven. When I hear your voice, all of the dogmatic, archaic perspectives of the world cease to exist. My love, at times like this, men have the habit of shutting down and dealing with problems externally. As a woman, there's something you should know. First of all, I'm sorry. You're attracted to me because of my outward appearance of strength. I must apologize, because those that appear to be the toughest are always the weakest. What I appreciate about you, my queen is that I am able to be 100 percent vulnerable with you. Men stuff inside their emotions, not knowing how to ask for help and feeling like they can fix everything. However, because you are my queen, I understand I must let go of that mind-set and hold on to you. Thank you for allowing me to just "be." Thank you for sticking through with my masculine, macho ideologies. Thank you for accepting me as I am.

You'll never have to worry about someone who is ALL in with the idea of building life with you. If you have those doubts and concerns there can only be two outcomes. This person is not the one, or you need to relax.

- Sylvester McNutt

Wonder Woman

You are indeed akin to Wonder Woman. You're a demigod, as she is. Your powers of "super strength, speed, agility, reflexes, stamina, and endurance" all make you respectable.

A woman who sacrifices, spends time and gives her soul to her loved ones is no wonder; this type of woman is actually the answer.

Please understand, that you are the truth; do not allow the lies that society has created shove you away from the self-love nirvana.

Queen, you are the star of this show and if you do not like the script, switch it up. You have the ability to add a new cast, change they story or end it and start a sequel at any point.

POETRY and Flaws

It's like the stormy days come back to back at the worst time. It's like "when it rains, it pours" feels more like "when it tornadoes, it hurricanes." The earthquakes of stress from life overwhelm me; the lightning strikes of confusion jolt me daily.

I try to manipulate the negative moments out of my life, but I'm overwhelmed by the inconsistencies of my own thoughts

And then…

You came and calmed the storm. You put stability on the ground that was shaking. You cleared up the gray skies. You wiped away all rain, wind, and heat. You made it okay for me to just be me.

You made it appropriate for me to be alive. You are my Storm. Yes, Queen, today we're going to have that tough conversation about your flaws.

FLAWS ARENT REAL

1) **YOU DON'T HAVE ANY FLAWS.** I'm not sure what part of your childhood instilled that in you, that you are not perfect as you are, but please acknowledge it.

2) **A VAST MAJORITY OF WOMEN PASS THEIR INSECURITIES ON TO THEIR DAUGHTERS.** Queen, can you objectively look at your mom and see if she possibly projected her insecurities onto you? (Remember that process occurs via behavior. An example of this is fear conditioning.)

3) **BEAUTY FLAWS?** Who are you comparing yourself to? More importantly, why, and even more importantly, who taught you to hate yourself? *Who taught you to hate yourself?* You don't have any flaws, Queen. Accept yourself so you can start loving yourself holistically.

**STOP ALLOWING
YOURSELF
TO THINK THAT FLAWS
ARE REAL.**

**WE ARE ALL DIFFERENT,
THEREFORE, THERE CAN
BE NO FLAWS.
STOP IT.
YOU ARE YOU.**

- Sylvester McNutt

Beauty Flaws Are Allusions

Queen, I'm okay with wanting to improve aesthetically. I may not understand the struggle you have fitting into regular jeans, or how uncomfortable your bra may be—I wouldn't, Queen, you're right. I do understand that it takes you over sixty minutes to put your "face" on.

Who taught you that behavior?

Why is there chemical after chemical that you play around with, as if you're composing a fine-arts masterpiece? Don't get me wrong; you're gorgeous either way. I accept you as you are, but Queen, who taught you to hate yourself? Is that true beauty, Queen? Why didn't your mother tell you that less is more, and your natural beauty will attract a person that cares about your heart?

Queen, you're trying to make yourself stand out from all these other women; you're trying to be the most attractive woman in the room. I get that, but that isn't real. In summary, Queen, you should just be yourself. Whoever taught you to acknowledge flaws should be removed from your life; you have none. There are 7.5 billion humans on this planet, and every single one of us has an issue. We are all just *unique*, not flawed. Queen, the last thing I want to tell you is that the more you love yourself first, the more love you can put in the world and the more love you can receive.

Preferences

There are two limits—pick one!

Hard limits: the shit you can't stand and will never be able to deal with.

Soft limits: the shit you can't stand but can tolerate in a relationship.

—Darnell Williams

Preferences

Basically, this married man was telling me to let go of expectation and the control factor. Just because somebody does something you do not like, that should not disqualify him or her from being your other half. No relationship is perfect. They all have problems, and the best thing you can do is accept that person for who he or she is.

This is a very important concept because a lot of women are single because their preferences are based in control and not acceptance. Just because you prefer a man with a beard, or one who has a "good job", that doesn't mean the man who is supposed to love you forever will have those traits. It's unfair to predict who your lover is going to be; you have to accept guys as they are. There is not a single man that can compete with fantasies of love that you have in your head.

Kiss Me like It's the First Time

Let it all go, my queen—any reason you
were ever mad with me. Let it go. I'm
asking you. It's a simple conclusion, but
you've allowed all of these thoughts to
confuse you.

Simplified, I love you, Queen. No, it's
bigger than love—I was *created* for you.

Kiss me like it's the first time.
Every time I kiss you, I kiss you like it's
the last time.

I'm grateful for the next times.
Your eyes are the color of the earth.

To me you are the world.
To me you are the sun and the moon.
I look up to you at night, wondering if
you can see me.

To me you are the galactic flares of love
across the universe,
The only thing shining when my world
is dark.
Kiss me like it's the first time, Queen.

Today, I run from any
form of abuse.
It can be physical,
emotional or verbal.

It is not my job to train
another adult to
understand what
respect is.

I care, I love you but
I'll pass on
That type of treatment
because
THAT'S NOT LOVE.

- SYLVESTER McNUTT

Emotional Abuse

I can speak to this because I was raised in a very emotionally abusive home, and I became an emotionally abusive person myself. I also attracted plenty of emotionally abused and/or abusive women. Yes, your culture becomes your culture. We raise kids to become products of their environments. If it wasn't for writing these books and the thousands of other poems I've written, I'm not sure I ever would have recovered from the dilapidated family dwelling that robbed me of my purity. My emotion of choice was anger.

I loved displaying my anger with a side of violence. By the time I was twenty-three, I'd been in over thirty street fights. I couldn't make these numbers up. In my freshman and sophomore years of high school combined, I had eighteen suspensions and forty-two days total missed via those suspensions. I went to counseling for almost four full years (as an adult, by choice) to understand and control this emotion. This was also the reason I started a spiritual journey about three years ago to fully understand myself.

I wanted to end the cycle and not carry that negativity into a relationship where my kids would feel and see that type of anger. A lot of the time, the people who are victims of physical, sexual, or emotional abuse allow themselves to be "victims" and never understand that the key is to forgive. (Of course, childhood abuse is different, because children don't understand it.) I can officially tell you that all of us have some type of emotional instability; that's not the issue. The issue is we don't objectively view ourselves enough, because 1) this culture doesn't allow us to accept ourselves, and 2) we never take the time to look inside of our own lives objectively without judgment. It really doesn't matter what "it" is. All that matters is that you're aware of what "it" is and you understand "it" and you take the steps to make sure it doesn't interfere with you having healthy relationships.

Today, **I run from emotionally abusive people**. Been there, done that. If you can't communicate with respect, you literally won't hear from me. The last side of that emotionally abusive thing is the fact that people don't separate themselves from the person causing them this harm. How many dudes do you know who stay with girls that nag them and curse them out all the time? How many girls do you know who stay with dudes that beat them, threaten them, and use their overbearing physical presence to keep a girl "in her place"? How many managers do you know that have to threaten you with "writing you up" or taking "corrective action"?

Well, Sylvester says, "Fuck all that. If you're not healthy for me, you're not for me. I've worked too damn hard to understand myself to deal with people who don't try and understand how their actions impact others."

Dear Queen: Come Home

You're wandering the world
with these damaged souls.

You're looking for love from
people who don't love themselves.

You're looking for love in people
who care about things?

You're not allowing love to find
you because you're living in this
vicious cycle of hate.

WAKE UP and get out of this cycle;
all cycles can end, all cycles can
stop.

All designs can be changed; you
have to make the shift.

Stand up for yourself, and get a
backbone; you have to do it for you.

September 2nd – Freedom

In order to appreciate freedom, you have to desire it. Love shouldn't enslave you; it should free you. It should power you as the sun does our solar system. Love should spark you.

The energy from your body should make sparks on the ground as you walk across carpet. Love should be present as the hairs raise on your forearms. Love is that feeling you get when you lock eyes and you instantly smile.

Love is that feeling where great desire mixes with a deep connection of belonging and acceptance. If you *feel* like you love them, then dammit, *love them*! Let them feel it so they can throw it back at you. We can and will break the cycle of hate with a massive amount of love.

September 3rd - Santa Monica Beach

She took charge like she was supposed to do, navigating the car, my energy, and my dimensions with every turn of the wheel. She never knew how much control she had over me.

Love wrapped me around her finger, and I was there to fill every little void that permeated her soul and left abysses like vacancies in her spirit. Jokers, looters, and gangsters came before me, robbing, stealing, and manipulating every miniscule part of her existence.

I became the reason for her survival, giving her verve and substance at every angle—lying on Santa Monica Beach, catching sunrays from the beam.
I build her up not for the moment of destruction, but for the moment of "no more voids," cutting the swords from the destroyed cord attached to our vertebrae.

She navigates the spaceship like she was supposed to, taking us away from other humans. The authority of two is enough to empower the flood of chemical amalgamation.

July 7th - Asylum

Our love - Entombed.
Asylum - Incarcerated.
I can't get gone, seduced up under your enchantment.

Lashing from heaven to hell,
This love has me going psychotic,
Doing things I've never thought of.
We make up just to break up.

This love goes through the flood.
You messed up my whole life like a hurricane.
Then you cleaned it up like Ajax.

Damn, why can't we get this right?
I don't want anybody else
And I'm tired of watching you waste time.
You're tired of me not being able to commit,
But I'm ready—but I said that last time…

You said last time was the last time,
But you keep coming back every time.
This asylum, ensnared, detained love, got us
muddled.
We don't even know if love is love anymore.

Women have all the power, but society wants to break their confidence and awareness. Men are controlled by women daily, but we've confused our woman into thinking this is not true. Men do what women allow, and women allow things based off of their perception of self. Hence why the message is self-love. Self-love determines how one will be treated in most situations.

- Sylvester McNutt

I sit here as a survivor of abuse.

Queen, this is why I write. I write because of the abuse I endured. I began writing because when I used to speak, I was lashed out at and responded to with aggressive behavior. In time I found myself in situations where I chose women who were just as emotionally abused as me, but we always lacked the skills to handle such strong emotions in efficient, healthy ways. Queen, don't step to me and idolize me, put me on a pedestal, or think I'm better than anyone. I'd love for you to respect me as the man that I am today, and in order for you to do that, you have to know it hasn't been all cake and punch for me. Not a victim, I'm a survivor; let's survive together.

My granny is always with me, and she hugs me and kisses me.

She never tells me that she misses me,
because I used my time wisely with her.
She is glad that my mother had me; life
was not really that hard.
Like 2Pac said, "It's only as complicated
as you make it to be."

Your family has no idea how hard it is to be you; your friends have expectations of the old you and have a hard time accepting the new one. It's like they don't see your changes.

I know it's a constant struggle you have, dodging the attention you don't desire, and I appreciate that you're dodging unsolicited attention left and right. One thing all people want is reciprocity, and I think it's necessary for you to know that there are no discrepancies in our mind-sets to resolve. Queen, I know that this world has sold you a vision that "falling" in love somehow equates to a successful, long-lasting relationship. I really have an entirely different angle with which to look at it that is much more radical. I hope you can accept that my goal is not to "fall in love." My goal is to develop a form of communication where we both feel heard, where we can go places without our cell phones, and where we can hit the gym together and let all of our negative energies out into it. I truly don't care about "falling in love"; I just care about getting along, having fun, and respecting each other. Falling does not sound like anything productive; it sounds like a pile of destruction collapsing because the base it was built upon could not handle it. Why would we seek to fall into anything? Instead let's accept my radical mindset of accelerating at love. I want to be the driver that pushes the engine of our love to the next speed, pushing beyond barriers and handling all the turns and curves with a doctor's preciseness. I want our love to be so steady that a surgeon's hands could not compete with the stillness of our security.

I know the ideology is a little radical, but it's completely logical to me, and I feel like it'll give us our best chance at creating a foundation that is unshakeable. So let's stand up in love and accelerate. Let's not fall in anything. Are you with me?

FALLING IN LOVE IS NOT MY GOAL, HOWEVER, FINDING

A WAY TO TREAT YOU WITH RESPECT, LISTEN TO YOU

AND GROW WITH YOU AS INDIVIDUALS AND AS A

COUPLE IS MY GOAL. FALLING IN LOVE SOUNDS FUN,

BUT THIS OTHER PLAN SOUNDS SUSTAINABLE. IF

"falling in love" OCCURS, THEN I WILL BE READY FOR

THE RIDE.

- Sylvester McNutt III #TheDearQueenJourney

There's something missing from your life. You're craving something real, something deep and rewarding. However, you have to stop blocking the blessing because of your fear of getting hurt.

If you want to find yourself and your love, then you have to stop going back to the joker that's been occupying your time. The joker can be your ex, an old flame, or the old mentality that's holding you back from the growth you need to get what you fully deserve. I understand how hard it is, because you care deeply about this person. Self-love and the love that you deserve will never hold you until you let go of the past pain. The person that broke you can fix you only if he's enhanced his skill and you've let go of the past. You have to remember that kings and jokers do not occupy the same space. If you want to build a kingdom with a king, you have to banish clowns from the kingdom. There's a gap in my life right now, and I would like to tell you about it. The gap has a lot to do with you not being here. I recently started writing this book for you. It's called *The Dear Queen Journey*, and it's about my plan to teach myself how to love. I just want to be transparent with you, because I hate trying to correct a lie. I do not want to lie anymore; I'm tired of feeling like I can't be honest and vulnerable. I'm tired of relationships with halfway commitments and behaviors, and that's literally only my fault. I couldn't fathom blaming anyone else. How is it that I am aware and conscious, yet I've allowed my past relationships to turn south via poor communication? Queen, I do not mean to bring up the past, but I want you to understand that I have to move forward differently from the way I was in the past. I hope you see that I'm just trying to figure this out too. I'm not here to force it, to manipulate, or to even try to prove anything to you. I feel like a queen is a woman who deserves to be treated with a high level of respect. My biggest desire is to find a baseline behavior and mind-set that is rooted in respect. I haven't always done that. I have not always kept my cool, and I don't know if it is possible. I've only been shown otherwise, meaning my life has been rooted in all forms of violence. I'm used to women yelling at me and telling me that I'm not good enough. Emasculation I know all too well, and it's something that I do not desire. What if it is possible? Well, if so, then I believe we are the ones who should do that. Why can't we just respect each other? Dear Queen, I want your input on this thought. Don't you think the other aspects of a relationship would be solidified and strengthened if we focused on respect? **In my observation, relationships are drastically missing the respect factor in their communication paradigms.** This is why we see couples arguing in public, making each other look foolish on social media, and why relationships these days are failing at an alarming rate. In order for us to understand respect, I'd like to introduce two different aspects of respect.

RESPECT IDEAS FOR HEALTHIER RELATIONSHIPS

PROJECTED RESPECT - This is when you give respect no matter what, and you project respect onto the other person that you're dealing with. An example of that would be this common situation: a couple is having a disagreement, and they separate for the evening. Projecting respect would entail a situation in which both people do not seek others for advice, do not make passive aggressive messages online via social media, and do not allow this moment of weakness to allow potential threats to enter their relationship.

LETTING GO OF NEGATIVITY - The main reason people jump into these modes of disrespect is because we naturally harvest negativity. We hold on to the images of pain, the feelings of resentment and bitterness. When we have these petty, weak, negative emotions, what happens is we approach people with these emotions, and they come off in the tone of our voice and actions. People are often guided in conversation by others' tone or message.

It's crucial that we submit to the idea of "letting go," simply because if we hold on to all of the negativity, then we will only create and perpetuate the cycle of negativity within our communication cycles with people.

Stop calling each other bitch and hoe; call each other Queens – Shift The Culture

I've called a woman a bitch before, and when I did it, it occurred because at that moment in time, I did not have any respect for her at all. I said it to hurt her feelings, to damage her, and to jolt her off her normal baseline of self. Now I refrain from using that word toward a woman.

I do not understand why women call one another bitches, It just doesn't seem appropriate to me. I feel like a woman who is constantly putting down other women, making fun of them, and calling them names is doing so because she has a deep, personal issue that she hasn't figured out yet. There's an underlying source of pain that has not been addressed, and I also feel like she's been indoctrinated in this behavior by society. I consider myself to be an enlightened, intellectual person with a diverse background of adversity.

I honestly cannot picture myself or any other man with a heightened sense of awareness actually having a desire to be with a woman that outwardly disrespects herself and other women like that. Honestly, that's not a behavior that I resonate with anymore at all. I picture that same woman using her potty mouth and jaded perception of her gender to spread that negativity to my daughter. I want more for myself and for my daughter. She does not deserve a mother who feels the need to lose her sense of respect by disrespecting other women in such an aggressive fashion. In conclusion, I no longer have a desire to call any woman a bitch at all on any level. I do believe that "bitching" is not exclusive to any sex. Bitching is just excessive complaining without accountability or awareness. Moving forward, **I hope you stop calling women bitches**. There could be a mass exodus of the word out of our vocabulary if we agree it is toxic and needs to change.

This woman on my mind is confusing. I don't understand why she doesn't see how beautiful she is. **I feel like she's lived a life of being judged by society, so my compliments on her beauty have literally no effect on her. How do I convince her that she's pretty just the way she is and that she does not need to change her physical appearance to please? I simply do not understand why our women feel like they have to compete with one another so much. Who taught them that dividing their power and bashing one another is the correct way to treat one another?** Don't women understand that men are naturally visual creatures, and we just appreciate looking at things we find beautiful? We observe other beautiful creatures, but that shouldn't engage an automatic self-defense feature. I guess I'll never be a woman, so maybe I'll never understand. She'll also never be a man, so I hope she can get this: men do not process your "flaws" or "insecurities" the way you do. In fact, we oftentimes literally think about only what we enjoy or like about you. The last thing we think about is what we don't like.

Starting this moment with a confession is fully necessary. A confession is a moment when you release the fear, judgment, and expectations of what you should be, and you just fully release your energy. In religion, they refer to a confession as an act of acknowledging your sins. I'm not asking you to do that; I'm just asking you to have a moment of transparency and honesty with yourself. I'm asking you not to blame the world, situation, or circumstance. **I'm asking you to find value in your past and not pain. It's not about looking back to see what you did "wrong."** It's about looking back to find places within your own behavior where you can learn and grow. *The Dear Queen Journey* is about growth, self-love, and learning how to love you first. One of the main goals of this book is to help readers find out what they are—not just today but every day in the future, because we evolve so often. I'm going to challenge you to make a confession to yourself only (you don't owe anyone anything). The purpose of the confession is to raise your awareness around your situations, your life, and your direction. You may be exactly where you want to be in life; if so, I applaud you. But one-day things will not add up, because that's just how life goes. When that day occurs, I'll challenge you to confess to yourself to give yourself the growth and healing that you deserve.

My confession: I, Sylvester McNutt III, have not always made the "right" decision. Now that I have learned mindfulness and practiced some non-duality awareness training, I believe that there is no such thing as doing "right" or "wrong." Removing the judgment of right or wrong allows you to see situations objectively. This is the true way to grow and learn from a situation, to actually learn from it by observing all aspects of it without your prejudice or biases based on your own personal judgment or interpretation of the "right" or "wrong" system. When you learn and/or teach people that certain behaviors and outcomes are right or wrong, you rob them of their free will to actually experience and observe the results of their and others' behavior. Understanding this process does not qualify the user to remove such moral standards as murder, physical force, or violence. **It's not a crutch to baby negative behavior; it's a reason to understand that objectiveness is the bridge to healing, accountability, and forward movement. I challenge you to make your own confession before moving forward, allowing the pain out and accepting the accountability aspect of it. This is how we heal.**

Rip Her Heart Out

I came here. I showed up on time. I showed up exactly when the schedule said to be here. They told me that if I came here right now, my queen would be right here in front of me.

Why do I have to find her inside of technology? Is she not real? Why do I have to send text messages to her? I want her to communicate directly with my atmosphere. I have a desire to reach down inside of her throat with my cold hand, grabbing her warm heart.

While holding her heart with my hand, I can feel the pain from the past throbbing through it. Enough is enough. I cannot repair this heart, and she does not know how. Fuck it. I rip her heart out of her chest and catch her limp body.

Her hair dangles over my arm. I drop the warm heart as it loses its pulse. To gain my queen, a sacrifice must be made. I understand that when a woman has her love needs met, she will pump life into a man. So I pierce my chest cavity, tearing my heart away from my sternum. I push my cold heart down her throat, forcing her windpipe to shift toward the outer cells of her neck. She comes back to life and catches me as I fall. To gain my queen, I have to give her my heart. Now she has a new one. Now she is pumping new life into me. Now she is complete again.

God-Like

Why did I have to go through that relationship? Was I supposed to feel all of that pain in order to absorb the pain that you were enduring simultaneously? Was I supposed to be near death because you were? I felt another soul rubbing against mine during that last tragedy I went through. Was it you I felt rubbing my soul with kindness from across the sky? I feel the hand of a god reaching down into my heart, the spirit of Apollo reaching over my energy, and the allure of Aphrodite taking over my tongue.

Died With

The true essence of your soul
Died with my poor decision.
If I could rehabilitate your heart, I would.
If I could sacrifice myself and absorb the
pain that
I bestowed upon you, I would.
If I could stop the internal waterfalls that
weigh you down, I would.
I can't imagine how you feel.
I'm so hurt and damaged by my own
decision.
I displaced an earthquake on your soul.
"I'm sorry" is not good enough.
"I'm sorry" means nothing.
I just hope time goes by, and I hope we can
learn forgiveness.
I do not deserve another chance at your soul.
However, we both know that our souls will
forever be connected.
I want to be the one to heal you, since I'm
the one that broke you.
I'll see you in a few years, and we will heal,
we will connect again.
We will grow and we will move past this,
even as friends.
Damn.

The Non-Physical Bond

"You should cherish the non-physical bond, sex shouldn't be a goal. It should only be an accessory to a connection. We live in a society that forces us to have sex without understanding our own emotions. Put value in the non-physical bond and knowing self, not value on throwing sex around hoping it lands us a ticket to love. Real love is enhanced when there is another connection besides our bodies. Sex releases oxytocin in our brain, and this chemical causes us to trust people more. It makes women pull down their barrier. This chemical does not determine the quality of the connection. It doesn't know if this is the king you've been praying for, or if he is just here to take your benefits. As men, we release dopamine when you we have an orgasm, which is directly connected to feeling pleasure. So, from a very basic level, women become attached and men become happy. This is why I stress to women the importance of a true, non-physical bond; you can hook a man with sex, but it won't be about love. You must develop a non-physical bond with him too. "

-Sylvester McNutt

BE SMART, EVERYONE cannot AND WILL NOT LOVE THE WAY THAT YOU LOVE. WE ALL HAVE DIFFERENT METHODS, HOWEVER, REMAIN AWARE AND NOTICE THE DIFFERENCE BETWEEN SOMEONE WHO LOVES DIFFERENT AND SOMEONE WHO JUST TAKES ADVANTAGE OF YOUR KINDESS, PAY ATTENTION

@SYLVESTER McNUTT

LET THAT

SHIT GO

- SYLVESTER McNUTT

<u>October 17th -Grey Area</u>

How can you not want me like I want you? What has happened?
Why do I struggle to get a minute of your time?
We used to always lie together and just stay napping.
Now every story I tell of you, it's saddening.
I wish I could honestly tell myself that I hate you.
I don't; I love you. But I wish I could replace you.
I can't, or maybe the reality is I won't.
But I should, because if you knew what I knew, you would.
Telling you I love you undermines the true feelings I possess for you.
I am head over sneakers, and I confess this to you.
I love you when you're near; I miss you when you're gone.
And when we're all alone, we get it on.
I love to hear you breathe. I love to hear you sing.
I love you so much I bought a diamond ring.
Couldn't afford it, but I made it happen.
I picture myself asking you and see you laughing.
They guaranteed us to fail, but we are winners.
You're the champ of my life. Dismiss all the other contenders.
You're my priority and my main focus.
But you don't want me, and I don't like the notion.
Every time I'm with you, I cherish the time.
I wish you would accept and stay with me for my lifetime.

The Girl I Never Had

If you could be my water, you would be the purest, most refreshing drink. If you were the question, I know I wouldn't be able to think or comprehend or even come up with an answer.

If you could be my rhythm and soul, I would be the smoothest dancer. You can count on me like a calculator. Don't subtract me from you; that would mess up the equation. You turned me, a boy, to a man, because it's so hard to say good-bye. I don't like crying, but I have no problem with this tear. When you are here, there is no problem, no danger or fear.

When I am away from you, I feel I'm incomplete, like a stamp with no letter; it's cold with no sweater. Let me lick my lips to get them wet and lick yours to get you wetter. Let me put my tongue in that spot that heats you up and gets you hot.

I question if I deserve you or not. I fucking love you; I don't like you a lot. You change my year like the summer equinox. I know you're warm when I am inside of you, like a pizza box. In my dreams she makes me forget of all of my exes, I feel like her name is Lexy.

These qualities exemplify the best woman imaginable. The sad part is I only see her with my eyes closed. I've never touched her or felt her face. We have never even stood in the same place.
This is the girl I have never met, the girl I have never had; the girl I only see in my dreams.

If you want a chance at someone's heart tell him or her with your words and actions. There is no reason to waste life, without love; take the chance you need at finding the person you see in your dreams.

Sometimes, it is love at first sight; sometimes you can be in love with a person after only knowing them for a few moments. It's possible that you may have to move for them. No matter what, remember that there is nothing more important than love; take the chance.

The person that broke you does not have the ability to fix you. I do not, nor shall I try. You deserve your time alone, and since you want to leave the house, I suppose I should allow you. I want you to heal and grow, even if that means I need to allow you to do it away from me. I'm willing to take the chance. The last thing I can do is sit around and wait for you to get over something. Sometimes when someone hurts us, that person becomes a symbol for the pain inside of our head. If I'm the representation of pain, then maybe not seeing me will result in you disconnecting the emotions of pain from me. The distance should allow us to heal and grow. I will wait for you. I do not expect you to wait for me, but I know your heart is with me, and you just need a little bit of space.

THE PERSON THAT BROKE YOU DOES

NOT HAVE THE ABILITY TO FIX YOU,

PERIOD. BUT, YOU CAN RECOVER

FROM A POOR SITUATION AND FIX

YOUR SELF.

@SYLVESTERMcNUTT

My Angel, My Love

My angel, my love, my other self
My dear, my heart, my equal half
My all, my motive, my strength
You are
My power, my pleasure, my pain
My smile, my laughter, my cry
My baby, my buddy, my love
The wind under my wing
The water underneath my fins
My cheeseburger, my cake, my onion rings
That's right, and you're my queen
My woman, my girl, my wife
I'm the keys to your piano chord
I'm the strings to your guitar
I'm the gas in our car, but you're the driver behind the wheel
You're the life that is born, beautiful and bright
My rouge, my jubilee, my storm
My DJ, my bass, the lyrics to the song
I'm your backbone, your support, your voice of reason
I'm your rodeo, your saddle, and I'm the horse
But you're the woman I love to wake up to
I love to hear your voice
We free each other like animals released from a zoo
You are the sock; I am the shoe
I am the thigh and calf
You are the blood and bones
You are my angel, my love, my other self
Finally, at last, I have love
Our hearts beat as one.
I will die for you, lie for you
You are my angel
Guide us; I just want to fly with you
I want to live life and die with you
You are my angel

Watching Her from Afar

She wants to escape the zone that she is in, feeling like multiple threats have been formed against her. She thinks that the antagonists are focused on destroying her, as rivals do. **She has a perspective of love that is not love. Her ex, her parents, and her view of society right now are so sullied. She doesn't trust anyone, terrified to show who she actually is. I want to close my eyes and see the stories that constantly run through her head. I want to see the flashbacks that will not leave her mind.** I want to know why she refuses to move forward. I want her to know that what she experienced was not love. It was a ball of emotions, a stagnant stage of her life that will not define her life but simply bring her perspective. I do not want her to go around hating men and saying that there are no good men. I wish she could see that men are struggling just as much as she is. I really hope that she let's go of the negative attitude, the fear, and the flashbacks of the past, because they are literally killing her soul and progress. There is a king somewhere, waiting for her to accept herself so he can love her. She may not see it, but she just needs to believe in something different.

Contemplating: Part 1

Let me take you to a zone,
A place real far, where your phone roams.
An unfamiliar place that's nothing like home.
They place you in a chair and take you out of
your throne.
Mouth says you love me; actions tell me that
you don't.
Understand my problems. You're right, but
you won't.
I can trick your mind to think you're my
clone.
Feel my cold heart and then shiver in my
bones.
Yelling loudly, "Please leave me alone!"
Taught to do right but I do everything that is
wrong.
I can't dance to the beat or sing to the song.
I question my life and say, "Why carry on?"
At the age of twenty-three, I didn't think I
would see this long.
When I made twenty, I was out on my own.
No family where I was. They didn't belong.
My mind in the gutter. Where had I flown?
Acting like a boy even though I'm grown.

Contemplating: Part 2

Take you out that zone and come into my brain.
I could sit here and talk about the pain,
Listen to the thunder, and talk about the rain.
You'll be hearing me, but you won't understand
Extraordinary love and nothing that is plain,
Like why I want to grow but I'm not willing to
     change
Or how people that I love I just lead on and let hang.
I'm always on a team but never in the game.
Because of my father, I've grown to hate my name.
If I could get surgery, I would embrace the change.
Just want to be accepted, but they label me as
     strange.
I'm sure I'd love a new life with a new face.
Maybe I'll actually respect a girl that I take out on a
     date.
I'm running all these routes, but I don't know my
     plays.
Flying to the love land. All the flights have been
     delayed.
If you never knew me, now I hope you can relate.
I hope that I have fun and all my problems fade.
People exiting my life, wishing they had stayed.
Progress on my mind, death in my face.
Maybe suicide is a solution, but what about the
     pace?
The pace of life is holding me down.
I don't know how to love a woman.
Why is there a void?

I wrote the contemplation piece about six years ago, before I published this book. I was at a moment of destruction. I wanted to die, period. I wanted to kill myself and end it all. **I was tired of being a child that was beat by his father and didn't understand the love from his mother**. I went to college just to destroy the hearts of women and use them for their bodies. I couldn't figure out why I couldn't truly value them. Yes, I had girlfriends that I tried my best with, but I couldn't give all of me because I barely wanted to be alive. Fitness and writing helped me maintain sanity during my life. My addictive personality and ways only continued because I literally wrote down everything, every feeling and emotion. I was in so much pain when I found out that she was sleeping with another dude. I was heartbroken and alone. I resonated only with anger. I sat in my 1992 Ford Taurus and thought about all the reasons I should stay alive. It was a cold night, and I was launched into a cornfield in DeKalb, Illinois. I never was good enough for any woman. When my high school sweetheart and I broke up, she messed around with my best guy friend the next day. Damn, was I not good enough? Were they secretly just waiting for the separation, or was it an impulsive charge of emotion? In college, the first girl I talked to lied and slept with one of my teammates. Then the second and third ones did the same thing. So now my sport of football I hate. I hate all football players, even though I was one. These dudes didn't care about any of them. They just wanted to use them to get their orgasm off, and I was trying my best just to figure out how to love each one of them. Women often think that all men are just "tough" assholes, but that's so false. We don't understand women at all. We don't understand why you allow guys around you when we're trying to build a connection. Do you really need an ego boost that badly? Each one of these women who emasculated me further deepened my insecurity of self. **Looking back, my biggest error was connecting my worth to others' perception of me.** Now and in the future, my worth is defined by me and me alone. I've found peace in trying to love myself holistically, consistently, and unequivocally. Now no woman's action can truly force me into those negative feelings. I suppose experience makes you grow wiser or colder, depending on how you view life. Perspective is everything; it's not about holding on to any of the pain from the past, regardless of how someone made you feel. It's about looking back and saying, "That was not love." Love does not do that to you, and it will not make you feel like that. If your story is similar, please believe me that those people in your past did not love you. There was just a web of emotion and growth there. It wasn't love. Remember that, and never lose yourself inside of someone else's perception of you. You are responsible for your own experience.

Her heart has run enough sprints at this point; she is ready for the marathon. But, she doesn't want to do it alone. She wants a partner who will help her run the race of her life.

-Sylvester McNutt

**JUST STOP
ARGUING WITH
PEOPLE.
WHAT IS THE
POINT?
YOU LOOK LIKE
AN IDIOT
BECAUSE YOU
CANNOT
CONTROL YOUR
EMOTIONS AND
COMMUNICATE
IN A CIVIL
MANNER,
CHILL.**

- SYLVESTER McNUTT

I know you're having a hard time trusting me because of what you went through in the past. Maybe I was the main source of your pain, and maybe I caused you trauma that you thought I could never cause you. Maybe it was the gentleman before me that corrupted you, and I'm just the collateral damage sitting here playing with only half of your heart. If I'm the source, I will be accountable for it and apologize deeply, but not with my words. I will apologize by curving my actions and the way we communicate to increase our odds of communicating effectively. The part that's killing me the most is that you don't believe anything I say. I can sense the fear, doubt, and insecurity creeping into your tone. It's so emasculating to me, because I am trying to fix something, but it's very possible that I must accept a deep reality, which is me knowing that the person who broke you cannot fix you. **Only you can fix you, through healing, letting go, and moving on from those feelings of the past.** I feel like you know exactly what you want, and honestly, I'm not sure if I am always what you want.

Knowing what you want in this situation is actually a problem, because you form an expectation of what you want instead of a cycle of acceptance. What you don't realize is that you've built up a wall around your heart that nobody can break down or repair. All I want to do is love you, so please tell me how. I'm begging for you to let me in. You're meaner to me than you realize, and then you're super sweet to your guy friends and family, so it just causes a bunch of confusion in my head. I really hope this letter helps. I'm not trying to tear you down. I just simply do not know how to tell you this. It burns me up on the inside, because I just want you to love me. I feel like women go through a phase of certainty and uncertainty. I feel like you're sure most of the time and unsure the rest of the time. It's like you want me around, but you're not sure at what capacity. I must tell you this: that is hard, and I don't know if I can survive that much longer. I truly love you from the bottom of my heart, and I can't keep up with the past anymore. I wish I had the answers. The past keeps creeping back in, and I will never win competing with the past. Is there any way we can just let it go and move forward? I've come to the conclusion that women love attention. I don't see anything wrong with that at all. Please go find me a person that does not desire attention. Attention is a great thing because it allows you to feel loved and wanted, like you belong. People who identify attention as a negative thing are weak to me. Yes, there are people who are so weak on the inside that they will do anything to gain the attention of others, even if they exploit their true self. That is not the kind of attention I am referring to. Having a goal to get attention from people you love or care about is normal, and acceptable to me. Stampeding horses thundering and shivering in the cold winter morning. The sun gleams and covers the blades of grass soaked with morning dew. Firewalls on the outskirts protect us as we navigate through the underbelly of the kingdom. Suddenly, the land that was once lightly tainted with a bright glare begins to grow dim. The earth starts to rumble as the clouds paint the sky a neutral color resembling the true color of my heart. We are being escorted in a gold-plated chariot. The universal law that I've found is if you don't give a good woman the attention she wants, she'll find it elsewhere. Women are patient too. They'll wait, but a good girl won't wait forever if your reason for a lack of attention is not valid in her eyes.

It's about balance, too. She needs to miss you, and you both need space, but in the absence of each other, she needs to know you're going to respect the relationship, and she wants you to be accountable for your time.

If you're at work all night and you can't reach out to her, eventually that void will be filled with another person. Best bet is if you're busy, send the good-morning text but put something behind it, and send at least one check-in during your work shift. She doesn't want a broke dude, so she knows you have to make that money, but at least give her a little time. Then at night give her quality time. Cut off the television. Cut off the cell phones. Do activities that have you eye-to-eye, heart to heart, and soul-to-soul.

The Hurricane Part 1

I never forget that night you left me
You should've stayed
You should have listened when I told
you to stay in the house
Now I have to recover
Your decision destroyed me,
destroyed us
Our love island was trouble free
Until you lost control
Until you lost discipline
Until you lost the value in me
Until you decided to run a hurricane
through my heart
And destroy everything that ever
resembled a soul
I'm beyond broken
Beyond damaged
Beyond jaded
Complacency settles, as life has no
meaning for me now
Where do we go from here?

The Hurricane Part 2

I left you that night because of all the
times you weren't there for me
I didn't want to stay because you
didn't want me there
You just didn't want to be alone
You have to recover? I was broken
first from this situation
I lost control
I lost discipline
The strength of my hurricane
destroyed your city
But your pollution polluted the earth
that made me create that devastating
spin cycle
Torn & terrified
Anger settles as life has no meaning
Where do we go from here?

Rain from the Hurricane

Rain from the hurricane drops all over my country. Seizures. Each step turns into a deep puddle of sorrow. It's too early in the morning to have the weight of the universe solely on my shoulders. Your poor decisions led to the strings in my heart tearing from their cell walls. My heart that used to play violin leads and deep harmonic echoes no longer carries that tune—the heart that was in desperate need of pure, harmonic energy.

Now my heart remains in a dilapidated state of worthlessness. The sole desire of my soul was to play the feature role next to a star. Now the light that used to shine bright has turned into a dim flashlight pointing its beam at the sun. The optic beam is so fierce and strong that my shadows have evaporated with heat from this pain. It pierces my soul so hard that my soul bends in half and cracks. I don't know if repairs to my heart are possible at this point. The emptiness resonates all too well. Welcome to my hurricane. Welcome to the catastrophe that you caused me.

Some nights I sit up caught up in random moments. Sometimes I feel so close to you but yet so far away. I'm dreaming of you every night, wide awake, in internal reflection on my soul and its growth, and it makes me wonder if I'll ever know your worth. I wonder if I value myself so lowly that I am too far gone from stable to extend a helping hand. Maybe I'm just being weak and acting like I'm dependent on you for validation. What if I'll never actually know you because I cannot value myself first? What if the key to this journey is for me to find the most value within myself, prior to meeting you?

Life presents us with these challenges, with questions and journeys that we go on. Oftentimes we never allow ourselves to truly uncover the answers or observe the ones that are presented to us because we anticipate how the movie will end. The human mind likes to alleviate pain in its experience by closing all gaps of uncertainty.

There's an allure to the mystery that is "life" that we must begin to embrace. We should stop limiting life to these walls of only what we know. When was the last time you embraced the mystery of change or the mystery of becoming a different version of yourself?

There's a prevalent amount of fear in all of us, which is necessary. Fear is the essential component of survival. Fear remains responsible for your fight-or-flight mechanism, which enables you to run from situations that will destroy, hurt, or manipulate your physiology.

So fear is not something we should run from, because we know it's necessary; it's only something that we should accept. It's something that we should understand. Fear is something that we should master; the mastery of fear will only lead us to an understanding of embracing the mystery.

These unknown factors also keep us at a distance from growth, but growth is essential for us to live. The word *evolution* is based on the root word *evolve*. It's just essential that we evolve consistently and regularly. The word *evolve* just means to develop gradually over time. Understanding that evolution is a part of life should help us accept that moving into the unknown is also a part of life. Think about it: Whatever you're doing now was at one point foreign to you, wasn't it? Again, there needs to be a balance of her just letting you go and accepting that you need to get busy, but you still need to make effort to let her know. Then at night give her quality time. Cut off the television, the cell phones. Do activities that will have you interacting eye to eye. There are so many simple tactics that you can try. Some women desire material possessions to make them feel good, such as flowers, gifts, or chocolates. In my personal opinion, those things can be effective but shouldn't be the primary way you show her love. I believe there can be a healthy mix of emotional support, attention, and gifts—all things that help her understand that she has your attention holistically, even if she doesn't because of the other pillars of life.

What Do Men Look for When They Are Successful, Good Looking, and Single?

1) THE GOLDEN KEY TO SUCCESS IS PEACE -A man who is serious about being in a relationship that will eventually blossom into a family desires *peace*. A peaceful woman is the most powerful accommodation a man will ever obtain. Most women in this generation are insecure and used to dysfunctional relationships—something about the '80s and '90s that really pushed our mind-set away from a level of comfort (I believe it was the increase in divorce and the rise of a hypersexual culture). Insecurity is relevant, because insecurity will lead a person directly into jealousy, resentment, and bitterness. All of those traits are the opposite of peace because they lead to arguments, breakups, and emasculation.

A secure man will only look for a secure woman. I believe that does not go both ways. I believe that a secure woman will look for an insecure man because she feels like she can "help" him or "save" him from himself. Unfortunately, she will add stress to her life, because it is not a woman's job to raise a man. The same goes for him if she is insecure. He does not have time to save or fix anyone's heart. The main reason for that is that most men do not feel comfortable repairing a heart that they didn't break; it really makes a man want to friend zone you and see you as nothing but a "hurt" woman. A man who genuinely has interest in starting a family does not care to endanger his children by choosing to deal with a person who has proven to be dangerous with her own heart and behavior.

I believe that every person in this culture has Insecurity. Having insecurity is not the issue; however, being insecure is a huge problem. **Having an insecurity is like running a mile with your shoe untied; eventually you will trip, but it will be okay, because you can just tie the shoe and fix the problem once aware of it, right? Trying to be with an insecure person is like trying to ice skate backward with Rollerblades on. Healing is required for the insecure person, who must let go of all the thoughts that keep him or her paralyzed in this insecure state.**

2) SUPPORT OVER CRITICISM - Most women have a bad habit of "trying to help everyone." I label it as a bad habit because most women are selfless givers, but they end up being around people who are takers. It's only a bad habit because they do not become conscious of it until time and pain have elapsed. Men need to be validated by feeling "heard," not

"corrected." A man will feel like a man if his woman supports him, meaning it does not matter to him if he succeeds or fails; all that matters to him is that his woman supported him along the way. The worst feeling is when you succeed and she didn't believe, because now you genuinely do not have an interest in sharing your new ideas or goals with her. The best is when she supports you win, lose, or draw. Correcting, adjusting, or saying anything petty that will make you look "right" and him look wrong causes separation and conflict. In other words, allow your man to fail on his own, knowing that he has your unconditional support. Men will oftentimes be wrong, but who is ever right in this world? There is no such thing as right or wrong when it comes to love. If it's love, then love is only experience and growth.

3) MEN ARE ATTRACTED TO MOST WOMEN THEY SEE - No matter how attractive you think you can make yourself with corsets, make-up, and other accessories, trust me when I tell you this: that stuff only matters to you. There is not a single man walking this planet that cares about any of that. This thought may seem farfetched to some women, but if you have any doubt, I challenge you to ask your male friends and brothers. If women really took a step back and observed the behavior of other women objectively, they would notice that it's women competing with other women for a

false sense of attention. I've said it over and over again, and I will take this thought to my grave. Men do not care about a woman's insecurities, ever. We never notice until she makes a big deal out of it. I dated this woman named Xena, and then I dated one named Dove. They were night and day by contrast, both crazy as hell. Okay, let me cut myself off, because a lot of people get called crazy now in this generation, and I want to reassure you that it's not craziness. What you have is a person who is overly passionate and a person who may not understand his or her passion. Xena was a diva, and you couldn't tell her anything.

She walked around like her shit didn't stink. Back to my point about insecurity: she exuded confidence more than any other trait, so to a man, it made her allure deeper. It made my attraction to her deeper because the law of attraction states that what you think about and believe dictates what your life will become. I put her on a pedestal because she put herself there first. My idea of her became what she projected of herself. She had insecurities, but we never really talked about them, and it was not a big deal for the relationship. I reassured her by telling her how much I loved her, giving her compliments and grabbing her booty everywhere we went. She had smaller boobs, and for some reason, I feel like women feel like that makes them less of a woman.

Just like she cannot control the cup size of her breast, I cannot control that I never even noticed it, because I was too infatuated with her small waist and booty shape. I was too in love with who she was and how she treated me.

Physically, I was in love with the shape of her face, her eyes, and her long brown hair. I literally never noticed that she felt like she was physically inadequate in that department. Truthfully, I do not know how she may have felt, but after speaking to her after the relationship, she let me know that I never added to her insecurity and that she knew I loved her unequivocally. Dove presented a different challenge to me. She was damaged emotionally and mentally from the last guy she was with, and she brought it into our relationship.

She told me from day one that she wasn't ready, and I didn't listen; I was hardheaded and knew that I could heal her. (Don't do that: if a person says she is not ready, then you should believe her, as opposed to making something else up or falling for the potential in her.) I spent the next two years trying to convince this woman of how beautiful she was to me, but she never tried to convince herself. Since she didn't believe it, I started not to believe it. I tried to love her, and I went into the relationship fully focused on her, but it wasn't enough. There is no person on this planet strong enough to save another person from his or her own negative self-talk. Let's live in reality for a moment: I am a man and an artist, so I appreciate beautiful things. I have observed women since I was four or five years old.

That's when I actually became conscious of the fact that there was a difference between boys and girls and that I liked making girls smile and enjoyed talking to them. I feel like some insecure people have this perception that you're only supposed to be physically attracted to one person once you decide to be with him or her. **Scientifically, that is impossible—you can't fight biology, and anybody that tells you otherwise is lost.** We have to accept that there will be others more attractive than us.

This does not mean it should equate to some inadequacy inside of us; it simply means that we are all ugly to somebody. Once you actually start looking at it like that, a certain peace will settle in. We are all ugly and gorgeous, so at what point do we stop being so hard on ourselves? At what point do we stop expecting other people to stop finding others attractive? As a guy, I am confident enough in my sexuality that I can notice when a good-looking, in-shape, or sharp-dressing man walks in the room. What do I look like, cowering up because of his energy? That makes me look weak. Instead I would encourage you to acknowledge it and show respect. If you're a male and another dude walks in while you're with your girl, there is nothing wrong with acknowledging his outfit: "Damn, bro, where did you get those shoes from? They are on point." Your girl will respect you because you can respect another. **You reach a moment of destruction once you say something petty or insecure**, like "He ain't shit" or "Those shoes are whack." The same thing goes for women. I'm going to give you guys the key.

Assume that your man is attracted to seven out of every ten women. If you see a girl with a nice booty and you know your man likes hump day, then acknowledge it. Do not make him feel silly because he looked at another human; it only shows insecurity and weakness. He will desire you more if you say something like, "Damn, her booty is on point." At first he probably won't know what to say, because it's "normal" for women to have this crazy expectation that men should only be looking at their wives. Okay, yes, there should be mutual respect too: if both people are out, nobody should be undressing another with his or her eyes. However, you must remember that people have free will, and they will do whatever they want anyway, regardless of your ideas of life.

Remember that *you* decided that you wanted to go back to this person and this situation, knowing everything that you know. So complaining about it is not acceptable.

Again, remember that *you* decided to go back. This means that you made a conscious decision, probably based off of emotion and potential. You remembered how it "used to be," and you wanted to get back to that. You also saw the potential in what this person "could" be. So you went back with a pissed-off attitude, expecting this person to change and looking for the potential in him or her, or hoping it would go back to the same way it once was. Sorry, sweetheart, but nothing in life ever stays the same. Have you ever heard of the word *evolution*? See, those expectations you have are killing you and your ability to see reality. Sticking around for "potential" is like trying to drink a cup of water and skydive: it might work, but you'll most likely make a mess all over yourself and continue plummeting toward the earth in a free fall until you splat against the ground. With that being said, the first step is letting go of whatever "reason" you have to act like an idiot and instead acting like a person who genuinely wants to move on from the negativity.

You're entitled to your feelings; however, you're not entitled to bringing up the past every single day if you claim that you want to move forward BECAUSE you're killing the relationship progress. Remember, you decided to come back, so you should decide to bring the best version of yourself to the relationship every single day. You have to reach peace with the past in order to stop bringing it up.

- SYLVESTER McNUTT

Why Do You Keep Going Back Expecting a Change?

In some cases the expectation of wanting another person to change is just as toxic as going back.

First you're going to blame the other person, because you're expecting this person to change, and that is simply not going to happen. It's unfair of you to place expectations on others, because they cannot meet your expectations. Remember that your expectations reflect the idealized behavior in your mind. **If you allow them to live organically, without force, then you will notice a change in behavior, because you'll be supporting real growth and giving that person free will. If you pester, control, and force a person to change, all you're doing is crippling his or her ability to really improve, because he or she is not being allowed to do this at his or her own pace.** Force only equals a plan to continue confusion, frustration, and misunderstanding. You've been hurt before, so now you feel like you need to control your interactions by micromanaging every little behavior, and that type of mind-set is further separating you from the peace and joy you deserve.

Step one is to let go of the expectation that another person will change and to recognize that we unknowingly push conflict by having expectations of others. The only expectations you should ever have are of yourself. If you expect a particular behavior of yourself, then you can always achieve it, because you can only control yourself. You cannot control stimuli, behavior, or opinions of others, ever.

Step two is to allow people to be as they are going to naturally be, without force, manipulation, or coercion from your words or behavior. This is the hardest struggle people have in relationships, because they feel like controlling the other person is going to promote his or her happiness. This person may appease you and meet your request because he or she is acting out of fear. Fear does not create adequate change or offer support for said improvement; it only provides a Band-Aid to the problem, and Band-Aids do not help healing. They just slow down the bleeding.

Finally, the last step is understanding that people do not grow at the same pace. No matter what you perceive to be true about another person's growth, you have to understand that people will grow at their own pace, which is based off of their experience, mind-set, and ability to feel accountability.

In summary, the key to growth is to stop expecting others to change. It's growth suicide, in my opinion, and will only garner you negative results.

Dear Xena

In order to find love again after heartbreak, you have to stop looking. You are love, but you'll never accept that until you understand that YOU are the one.

NOT THEM, BUT YOU.

@SYLVESTERMcNUTT

In order for me to complete *The Dear Queen Journey*, I have to write you a few letters. **I need closure. I need to express how I feel and think about you.** It's important that while telling this story of love, I mention the first person who I ever felt loved me, which is you, Xena. This part of the story is going to be transparent, honest, and vulnerable. So let's get it started. First and foremost, I love you. When I say I love you, to me it means a lot. I do not believe love is something we can truly define. I think its shape is formed like a spiral and gets manipulated as life goes on. Visually, I see love in the way a football gets tossed in the air from one person's hands to another's. It's a transfer of energy, if you will. I notice that some football passes have very tight spirals and are very compact and precise with their delivery. However, some football passes are ugly, and the ball is wobbly. As we learn, absorb pain, and shift through life, our perspective changes. I've never lost sight of loving you, ever. When I first met you, I was in awe of how gorgeous you were. I remember seeing you walk in the doorway to my house the first time.

You weren't there for me, though; you were dating my roommate at the time. I've always appreciated beauty, but when you walked in, it was different. **I actually felt your energy and spirit simultaneously as I saw your hair draping down over your shoulder blades. I felt how damaged you were. I saw how you were masking it inside of that crooked smile.** I never imagined that a girl with your beauty could see anything in me at all. I was so weak and broken when I met you that I had no perception of self-love. I'll never forget watching you walk with your wide hips and skinny waist, as your hair ran down your back like a farm of ants. Your eyes were the color of the earth, blue and green at the same time. Your smile captivated every single room you were in and made my heart freeze in time. I literally fell in love with you the minute I saw you. It was love at first sight. I was so shy and insecure. I knew for sure that you would never notice me. I had nothing to offer you, and you had family, ambition, and heart. I was semi jealous of you and your life, and for you to see value in me was just plain confusing but empowering as well. You loved me as I was from day one. You never tried to change me; your encouragement deepened the love I had for you because it built up my weaknesses. It was unreal for me to have a woman meet me and then accept me for the person that I was. I wasn't used to being treated like that. You thought I was smart, funny, and attractive. I remember you telling me, "I wasn't attracted to you when we first met, but I became attracted to you after I talked to you." Secretly, a bit of insecurity set in when you first told me that, but then the more I dwelled on it, the more I realized that you becoming attracted to me the person was far more valuable than you being attracted to solely my appearance. My mother loved me very much, but as I grew a bit older, I became distant from the emotions that I needed from a woman, simply because our relationship had changed. Once she and my father split, she was no longer around, and I became very distant from women. I grew cold. I believe I was absorbing some of the pain my father had from my mother leaving. Meeting you was unexpected, and it was necessary for my growth. Xena, this was the beginning of us. This is how we started. Now sit back with me as I take you through our relationship, thoughts, and feelings. I believe we both can learn from revisiting it all. I believe our story can influence others to love more, to love boldly, and to appreciate what they have. I believe that the clarity I have now, looking back on our interactions, can literally save and change every relationship that has struggles. Between you and me, we taught each other how to be in a relationship, and the gift of what we shared will now live forever. Due to your support and belief in me, now we can inspire, help, and encourage other couples who may need it. It's ironic to me that I am writing this book called *The Dear Queen Journey*, because you were the first queen that I started writing to. No matter what happens in life, understand that I will always care for you and will always desire the best for you

Dear Xena,

Why was I in fear? When we first met, I was scared to touch you. Why was I scared to commit, be transparent, or be intimate with you? You never asked me these things. You literally just accepted me as I was, but I bet you thought about it. I bet you thought about why I couldn't be open and honest with you, or why it took me so long to start trying.

CLOSURE IS INTERNAL, IT HAPPENS RIGHT AFTER YOU ACCEPT THAT LETTTING GO AND MOVING ON IS MORE IMPORTANT THAN PROJECTING A FANTASY OF HOW THE RELATIONSHIP COULD HAVE BEEN.

- SYLVESTER McNUTT

Let's touch on this situation, the scared-to-commit situation. The way our relationship worked out, I had no choice but to commit, because at the time we literally needed each other. We became a support system for each other really quickly due to circumstance. My apartment became a safe haven for you to get away from the stress of life, or should I say your mother. You had constant pressure from your friends and family, and their desire to use you wore your powers thin. It was like coming over to see me gave you a sense of peace and serenity that you couldn't get out in the real world. We had the same pain when we met each other. We both had a lot of anger and resentment toward our parents. For me, I was angry with my father, and you were angry with your mother. It was hard for me to have the distance and literally no communication with you, and for you to be in her face every day and have dysfunctional communication with her. Our bond was built on our desire to be loved and accepted for the people that we were, since we were not receiving that from our parents.

Dear Xena, Part of what helped me fall in love with you so quickly was your personality. I had never ever met another person like you. Your drive and passion was literally unmatched at the time. I was attracted to you because you were passionate like me, but you didn't have problems showing it. The goddess abilities you had that really captivated my soul were your abilities to multitask and to lead people. I always envisioned that my wife would be a woman who could lead, with or without my influence. Oftentimes I am the leader, so for me, part of my quest has always been to find a woman that I can submit my leadership role to when the situation permits.

I fell in love with you because I idolized you; I put you on a pedestal. It was easy for me to fall in love with you, because our relationship got serious fast. We were making each other breakfast (me cooking for you) very quickly. I remember you helping me organize my closet, and we had just met. What I loved about you the most was your desire to please your family and me. You've always been the type of person to put forth maximum effort. To see you try so hard at our relationship, in school, and with your family was motivating for me. I never wanted to give up or quit anything, because your energy was so pure and motivating.

I'm guilty of idolizing you and viewing you like a celebrity. I was lucky to know you, and for you to get that close to me was literally one of the biggest surprises of my life.

Putting Someone on a Pedestal

We are all guilty of this behavior when we truly care about someone. We glorify that person and put him or her up on a pedestal, which is great to grow and to show how much you care. However, there is one problem that always occurs: this person often gets away with different behaviors because he or she is on a pedestal. We glorify this person. We make it seem like this person is perfect and can do no wrong. If I could go back and give myself knowledge, I would tell myself how you can still respect the person you're dating and honor her without putting them on a pedestal. It's not that you didn't deserve to be there. Honestly, I didn't deserve to allow you to be there, because I just went with the flow even when things didn't add up or make any sense to me. I turned a blind eye to the problems because I cared so much, and that technique is weak and lacks accountability. Wherever accountability lacks, so do results and growth.

ELEVATE YOUR PARTNER TO
THE HIGHEST LIGHT,
HOWEVER, YOU SHOULD
NEVER PUT THEM IN A PLACE
THAT DOESN'T ALLOW YOU
TO HOLD THEM
ACCOUNTBALE FOR THEIR
DISCREPANCIES AS WELL.
RELATIONSHIPS PROSPER
WITH ACCOUNTABILITY
FROM BOTH SIDES.
             - SYLVESTER McNUTT

I know why we were successful in our relationship. It was because we needed each other at the time, due to our family hardships and financial struggles too. We were both poor college kids who came from struggle, just trying to find a way, constantly matching each other's effort and energy. We were both in a lane of pain due to the circumstances of our parents, due to the errors in the ways people decided to treat us. The best aspect of being with another broken person is when that metamorphosis happens, as the two try to grow together. For us, we loved each other, but we also loved the idea of each other. That was our gift and our curse; it was the thing that brought us together and partly the thing that pushed us apart. You recently shared with me that I used you while we were dating, because I needed you. I for sure felt used by you as well. I felt like I was just a place of peace for you, and like I was a stepping-stone for the next big thing. **Objectively, we were both insecure within ourselves, and that contributes to that "being used" feeling.** If we could go back in time and do the relationship over, I would have a desire to show more appreciation and to validate your feelings more. I didn't have the skills then to understand how important it is to validate your woman's feelings. I've noticed that with women, when they say how they feel or how they think, they're not actually looking for solutions. They're looking for validation by reassurance and understanding, not necessarily solutions. I made that mistake often with you. I was not good at reassuring you or letting you know I understood you. Offering solutions is not the answer women look for. Oftentimes they will come to their own conclusions. It's just that women want to be heard. That's how they express themselves. They understand their feelings and thoughts by talking about them, not by looking for guidance. My recommendation for anyone is to pay close attention to this behavior. You can learn from my interactions with Xena that reassurance and understanding are more important than making suggestions.

I used to look you in your brown eyes and see directly into the capsules of love that you would swallow for me every day. You genuinely loved me to the maximum capability that your heart would allow. When you looked back into the abyss of my soul, I hope you saw that I tried to love you too. The problem for us was that we loved each other and that everyone else around us hated us being together, including us. We had a relationship of love with no love, simply because we did not fully love ourselves. I didn't love myself, nor was my identity structured enough to support the idea of carrying your soul with me through eternity. I lacked self-love. I was just a poor man with heart and ambition. You were just a fragile little girl who felt like she needed to be strong because she was so weak. We were the toughest people outwardly, but weak and awkward intrinsically. Xena, I hope that you continue to practice loving yourself by making the best decisions you can with your body, mind, and health. We've talked extensively, and then we don't speak for a time. It's the cycle of what our friendship has become. I hope you continue to embrace *The Dear Queen Journey*, which is the journey of personal self-discovery and self-love. It's not about you finding a man—nor is it about me finding a woman. The journey is about us finding self-love, and I am so grateful that I know you, because without our experiences, I don't think I would be here today in this position. I truly love myself, and some of what I became I took from you and amplified. Xena, **why were we so destructive toward each other while claiming we loved each other? It was a sick, addicting love, the parasite on my existence—and yours, I'm sure.** My goal for you and others it to let go of all the pain, fear, and insecurity from the past and allow the love of self to replace the void that previous relationships have left. We all deserve love. However, we expect it from others, and the only way people will love us is if they are full of love themselves, or if we internally love and then allow others to send us their versions of love.

Why Is There Pain After a Breakup?

Sitting with the emotion of rejection or abandonment can literally make you go crazy and forget about self-love, your thoughts turn into self-hate after a breakup.

Xena, we broke up and got back together at least fifty times, so writing about this subject is really easy for me. I hope you find some humor and truth in these thoughts here.

The Minor Breakup: This occurs because you can't control your anger and decide to break up with me. The reason for this minor breakup is not that you actually want to break up. It's that you're actually begging for me to give you more attention or to soothe your confusion. The only reason you actually break up with me is that your confusion overwhelms you, and you are aware of how much I care. You truly have no intention of breaking up with me; your indirect goal is to pull me closer. This break occurs usually because there was a miscommunication somewhere in the process.

How the Minor Breakup Makes Me Feel: Well, since you introduced the breakup with anger, and because it's an emotional outburst, what I do is react with anger. This is one of the biggest problems that people have in relationships. Instead of responding with clarity and understanding, we match each other's emotions. This is singlehandedly one of the most toxic behaviors that can exist in a relationship. If you think about it objectively, just think about this: I'm angry. I yell at you. And then you're angry, so you yell back. My question is where is the progress? Both people are exhibiting behaviors that are not conducive to having a successful relationship.

The last thing you need to do is focus on changing anyone. Your goal should be to accept people as they are. That will enable them to grow at their own pace, and it will enable you to appreciate them as they are. If you expect anyone to change, you're ruining your ability to love this person, and more importantly, you are only setting yourself up for failure. Our society has a messed-up perception of love being this fairy-tale external emotion. Love is a normal emotion that you should feel every day from coworkers, friends, and family. Focusing on finding love or creating love is the wrong angle. Love is an organic entity that lives inside of every single one of us. The search should only occur internally, especially since love's values are 100 percent intrinsic.

You would not search for donuts and candy at a health food shop, would you? If you walked into Whole Foods, you would search for healthy, organic food. This should be your view of self: that you are the healthy, organic idea or version of love. You should view yourself as an organic grocery store—because you want the organic, healthy version of love, correct? You need to stop bringing donuts (toxic, negative, or bitter behaviors or people) into a place of health, then.

Every day that you wake up, you're faced with a choice of which package you want to bring to the table. When you go to a car wash, they present you with four or five different packages that you can select. Most people automatically select the package within their budget, or the cheapest. That logic does not make any sense to me at all. Why are you going to go wash your car without using the best way to clean it?

We also continue this behavior in life. We think about our "life budget" instead of thinking about our "life value." Ideally, you should select the highest package every single time—not because it's expensive, but because it has the most value. Value is the determining factor for success in all channels of life. In my last book, *Success Is a Choice*, I talked about how the people who have the happiest lives, impact others, and shift the culture are people who "add the most value, every single time" to themselves, their environments, and others.

If you're dating someone, please remember that you have a choice to make every single day when you wake up. You can wake up and deliver a lower-grade package to this person, or you can wake up and send him or her a package with your best bundle. A bundle that's going to produce success in your relationship is one where you release pain from the past, practice forgiveness, and enable your listening and empathic skills as you seek to grow and learn with this person. Picking a lower package would mean you're bringing this person your fear, insecurity, or unnecessary baggage. The true essence of choice is realizing and accepting that you're accountable for all actions and outcomes. There is no reason to blame everyone or anyone, especially if you're not giving your best package. You're the one to blame—be accountable.

Your life is solely about your life. You are the one responsible for your experience and emotions. Nobody else can save you from yourself; Superman and Wonder Woman do not actually exist. They are indeed fictional characters of someone else's fantasy.

Today I challenge you to decide what your best package is, and I challenge you to figure out how you can bring your best package to that table for your own benefit every single day. What qualities, skills, and attributes do you have? What is a benefit of knowing you? What do you like about yourself? Why are you going to do better today than you did five years ago?

Notice how all of these questions require positive answers? It's not about looking for weakness or negativity within your package. It's only about understanding what you are, who you are, and your plan to deliver your best for yourself. I say "for yourself" because you are your own motivation. You deserve happiness; you deserve bliss and success every single day.

In conclusion, I want you to accept my challenge and figure out what your best package is right now. No more time can be wasted squandering away your life and time. Life is about value, so let's focus on developing your "value package." If there are any negative, bitter, or toxic people or behaviors that are influencing your chances at success and bliss, please understand that you need to cut them off, immediately.

The most important thing I can do for myself today is understand who I am. This society has a glaring hole of inadequacy that we force upon our children. The biggest two problems we have, which we can fix damn near immediately, are the beauty expectations we place on women and the fear we instill in our men around "being emotional" and showing "weakness."

It's so important that we strive to accept and understand who we are, because society is established right now around attention. Everything revolves around attention. Businesses need attention, women need attention, and everything is run by who can get the most attention. Attention is the driving factor for life in this generation. This is why we stress out women—because we pressure them to think they need attention to feel acceptable. In nature, the peacock with the brightest, most vibrant colors is the one who attracts the most male suitors. In our society we attempt to duplicate nature; however, we duplicate aspects of self-hate all too often.

We have a generation of little girls convinced that the true power of a woman is embedded inside of her physical appearance. The same applies for this generation of men. We have it lodged in their brains that showing emotion equates to weakness. We have our young boys thinking that crying is "weak." Crying is a perfectly normal human reaction, so my question is how did we fall so far away from reality that we expect grown men to subtract this normal behavior from their dichotomy? As a man, I can tell you that I'm super attracted to a woman of confidence. I personally do not notice a lot of the insecurities that women mention as their "flaws." It simply does not register with me as a male.

When a woman walks by me, I observe one thousand things I like about her, some physical and some related to her behavior. I think women have this perspective that men are all "breast" or "booty" types of guys. I think we see those things, of course, but I notice things about a woman like hands, her hair, or her eyes. These things stick out because they are intrinsic qualities. Just because my intrinsic beauty qualities do not necessarily align with what she thinks is beautiful about her does not negate her beauty. As humans we are all unique, and this is what makes us unique: our ability to have different features. I want to be blunt here, and I hope not to offend anyone. I just want to help clear confusion. I, Sylvester McNutt III, have been attracted to all races. I believe that all of the women in this world are gorgeous. I have dated black, white, Latino, Middle Eastern, and Asian women.

The commonality between all women is that they are women. The differences in them are not flaws; they're just differences. Differences make people special and unique, not fragile and weak.

I am personally challenging all of the women who read this to accept this ideology. The same challenge goes for men who do not feel like they can be vulnerable and honest with their emotions. Men have the expectation of strength, yet true strength relies on your ability to improve from, bounce back, or resist a negative force. The modern-day man is out of touch with his emotions because he plays games growing up that instill physical violence by teaching him that men should brutalize one another. I'll never forget playing football in the backyard neighborhoods of Chicago, Illinois, and how rough and violent we were with one another. I can't forget the yelling, screaming, and physical attacks that we displayed all in the name of a game. Logically, when you think about it, there's no sense behind such behavior. Yet those moments playing in the yard, fighting with other kids, and running races in which the loser would get made fun of and emasculated literally defined my childhood. A lot of the same things are found in today's society, but with the advancement of video games and social media, now young boys are competing in professional gaming tournaments and competing for popularity as well on social networks.

One day you will wake up and understand that you have literally no control over your life. The day that you give up the false sense of control and security, a serene calm will set in. You'll appreciate different aspects of your life that you never did before. The barriers that you've established to protect your heart will turn into freeways of calm, peace, and love. Until you let go and allow peace, self-love, and self-awareness to settle in, you will remain on rocky terms with yourself. You will continue your slavery to nothing. Free your mind.

Dove, there was a time when all I wanted to do was love you by showing you affection. I used to care about your mood and how you felt. It's possible that I cared more about you than me. That was my fault. I sacrificed loving myself to try and love you. I failed consistently at this relationship thing with you because I was so far gone from understanding and accepting myself. If I could go back, in retrospect I would tell you that you were a cancer for my happiness. I would tell you that I was the devil in a cloak.

   I would tell you not to respond to my text messages and phone calls and to keep curving me like you did. I should have listened to you when you told me you weren't ready. I remember you crying after dinner in the restaurant, and you were telling me how you weren't ready and you were broken. Of course, I took on the Superman attitude, and I knew I could save you—but that was the demise of our relationship. If I could go back to younger me, I would say,

   "Hey, you need to let her go, brother. You need to allow that woman to heal under her own pretenses. Why in the world would you save her when she is not even ready to save herself, and who gave you the support to consider that you were that special to save another person?" One month removed from your grandmother's passing, and you actually thought you were ready to move on? Yet just months before, you were hooking up with the Latina woman every weekend and blowing money in nightclubs. I believe you thought you were ready, but you weren't actually ready. I think you tried hard to make that woman happy in the beginning, and eventually you ran out of energy. I remember you telling the Latina girl that you found someone new and that you wanted to build with her. In retrospect, I respect that move, because you wanted to be faithful and give this new girl a fair chance at your heart. Sylvester, honestly, you did all the right things with her, because you cut off the other girl immediately, and you put a lot of effort into calling her and being available. Next time you get in a similar situation, I want you to listen to the woman if she says, 'I'm not ready.' That may be her way to cry for more effort; however, there is truth in every word a person says. If she is not ready, you cannot make her ready. You simply have to allow her the time and space she needs to grow and heal appropriately. As a result of not listening, you entered a relationship with someone who was full of passion and energy but who did not possess the filter and control to navigate her love efficiently." I don't fault her for us not working out. I take full accountability for my contributions. I believe there was a process that happened that eventually killed our source of love. Let's go deeper.

The Broken Mindset

1) **TWO BROKEN PEOPLE CANNOT FIX EACH OTHER** - I found you a week after my grandmother died. I was so broken and empty on the inside because of losing her. I was already jaded and petrified because of my exchanges with Xena. I was naïve and believed I was ready because I was "strong," but I was still broken from the breakup with Xena. We were so broken that we couldn't identify our brokenness. We were both collateral damage from our previous interactions. I wish we would have known this to start, but two broken people cannot fix each other. Healing is an eternal job, and nearly

every one of us is horrified to leap into the abyss of our self to find out who we really are.

2) **THE BROKEN PERSPECTIVE** - I hope that the readers of my material understand that **no matter how much passion and desire two people have, if they are not comfortable within their own selves physically, emotionally, and spiritually, failure is inevitable.** The course of loving thyself is more important than seeking love from another. This was a perfect example of how broken people ruin broken people. I said something a while back that resonates with this. I believe my exact words were, "Broken people are so broken that they are too broken to identify their brokenness."

3) **HEALING** - "I am not ready to be with you or anyone." Why do we not listen when people speak? We must activate our listening skills and understand that broken people

literally always show you that they are broken. I've used the word "broken" a lot in this section, so let's get on the same baseline for the sake of understanding and consistency. I believe a broken person is a person who has encountered a traumatic experience; however, he or she still has unsettled emotions connected to said experience that affect his or her normal plane of thought daily. I believe that we victimize ourselves all too often by explaining and detailing the stories of the past. I believe we connect our present-day worth to the things that have happened to us previously. We are broken because we subject ourselves to subjective logic, which cannot exist because logic is objective. We assign meaning to everything, and those same stories are the screenplays that direct our souls toward bliss or hell. I believe the key is to let go of everything, especially trying to understand other people's behaviors. There can be nothing gained if we blame others or allow our emotions to control us in said situations. I am not asking you to be stoic and robot-like in your ways. I believe that having a clear conscience around your previous situations is the easiest way to heal. Healing is the process of letting go of the stories and pain. Is it easy? No, it's not easy at all, but life is not about being easy; it's about trying to understand. The key is to understand that you may not understand everything.

4) **SACRIFICE AND EXCUSES** - I think the greatest thing that I learned from Dove was sacrifice and letting go of excuses. Here is how I learned that lesson. When Dove and I met, she lived sixty-five miles away from me. That was well over an hour in the car and at least a quarter tank of gas. Dove was so interested in me that she would drive to my house after work every day, which was sixty-five miles. She sacrificed her time and her gas, and she never made excuses for her choice. I

noticed that she never pushed it in my face either. She never made me feel bad because she was putting in the effort to drive to me. Yes, I drove to her, but nowhere near as often as she would drive to me. **As a man, I felt like it was my responsibility to make sure her drive was worth her time. I made sure I invested all of my focus into her; I would not play on my phone or be distracted by meaningless things. I gave her my undivided attention and tailored her experience with me to her. We would go on long walks around the neighborhood, go to parks, and go to restaurants. I always made sure we went out on dates—the movies, dinner, and bowling. My biggest goal was to make sure I gave her a good experience with me, and even if it was just us lying around the house, I wanted her to feel like her effort was matched.** I would like any of my readers to pull knowledge from this situation and understand some of the behaviors we used. I believe it was very valuable that neither of us threw things in the face of the other person around "effort." We both just tried as much as we could, even though our efforts were different. The first six months of the relationship were like this, and I thought I was going to marry her—I really did. Then I moved, and the relationship with Dove and I went downhill. I suppose this would be a good time to talk about how to be successful in a long-distance relationship.

Long-Distance Relationships

Dove, if I could go back in time, I would give us this perspective. I truly believe that if we would have stuck to these simple thoughts, everything would have been okay.

1) COMMUNICATION - In times when distance is great, communication must also be great. When you're together with someone, you can literally sit with him or her for hours and not speak; that's just the power of a bond. Words are not always necessary. Sometimes people just want to be around and hold a person, or lay on each other. When you are in an LDR (long-distance relationship), the only thing you have is communication. Now, this is great because technology is so far advanced that we literally have hundreds of options, like Skype,

Face Time, text messaging, social networking, phone calls, letters in the mail, and e-mail. I suggest that people utilize all of them. Let's be honest: Most people have jobs and hobbies, right? So texting and e-mail are great for that. Conversations need to occur frequently because that's how you connect with a person's tone and mood. Lastly, the video-chat service is important because it allows you to see that person's smile. I believe that you should connect holistically via all of the possible solutions. Communication is the most important factor, and even if you guys are just sitting there looking at each other on a video chat, it's okay. Sometimes you just need that person so you do not feel alone.

2)   TEMPTATION - The biggest threat to the relationship from a long-distance perspective is the temptation of others' attention. You have to know this going into it, and knowing this won't produce fear; it will help you produce a plan. It will help you

have those tough conversations about who you are with and what you are doing, because it's more important now to be really open, unlike if you were with the person every day. When proximity is a problem, different insecurities and jealousies can permeate the relationship, and that is normal. Both people have to be humble and mature enough to accept and respect that. It means we have to be more vulnerable and honest. If there is a threat to the relationship, it means we need to either nip it in the bud or be completely transparent with the person. It also means that the guy will need tons of pictures and videos of you. Women downplay this because they don't understand the psychology of a man, but have you ever wondered why a man will make this statement—"Send me a picture"? He does this because seeing you helps him connect and feel like he is there with you. The woman just wants to hear his voice, but the man is concerned with seeing her. It makes him feel like the woman is claiming him by showing him a picture of her.

One of the keys to being with a man is to understand that he is driven by temptation. So be his temptation every day of the week, versus being a version of conflict by assuming another woman has the opportunity that you were born for. As men, we are driven by visuals; we want to see our woman in fancy ways. Each man has a different perspective of what fancy is for him, but don't forget to wow him sometimes. Remember, he initially was attracted to you because of the way you looked. After a while, he got to know your soul.

The Moment of Self-Love

"SELF-LOVE IS ABOUT BEING OKAY WITH NOT BEING OKAY. IT'S ABOUT LETTING GO OF THE SELF-JUDGEMENT. "

- SYLVESTER MCNUTT

Walking through the local organic grocery store listening to Mariah Carey's "Breakdown," and I lost it. I burst into tears. I lost my cool and allowed the tears to just flow. I was weeping inside of a public store, but I felt like there was nobody in the store. I felt alive, organic, and raw. I was empowered by my journey. I was so happy; it was the first time that I actually realized that it was okay to love myself. This was the moment of self-love for me, the moment that I fell in love with myself. Tears dropped off my face, and I couldn't hold my basket of fruit. For that moment I had no desires, no wants or needs. The only thing that mattered was my mindfulness in that present moment. The tears kept rolling down my face as a grin took over, and I smiled from ear to ear. I could feel my heart slowly transfer blood throughout my body. **Time completely stopped, and all of the hormones in my body went away. It felt like the moment I'd been seeking the entire time on this journey.** *The Dear Queen Journey* was never about finding another person; it was only about finding me inside of myself. It was about accepting that no matter what I have gone through or will go through, I will be okay. It was me fully understanding that loving myself is the most important factor in life. This journey was about letting go of the past and moving forward—trying to understand why past relationships didn't work out so I could learn objectively from them. It was about accepting that the person you will love forever has to love herself, and if we want anyone to love us, we should practice self-love. This journey is about respecting your exes and parents and not harboring any negativity or hate toward them, because those feelings only enslave us to the past. This is *The Dear Queen Journey*, and you are now a different person after reading this. **My challenge to you is to deepen your relationship with yourself by challenging your current mind-set and ideologies. I want you to critically think about everything you've been through, removing all judgment and biases. I want you to see everything from others' perspectives and see how they could have benefited if your behavior or mind-set were different.** I challenge you to never disrespect love again, because now you are love. I challenge you to deepen your relationship with God or with your universe. Regardless of what you believe in, just commit yourself to learning and love and being love. You'll never fall in love after reading this book; you will stand up in it forever. As the tears stream down my face writing my last chapter, I want to make one request of every reader. The last request I have of you is that you enable love inside of yourself with no equivocations, with no conditions, and holistically devote yourself to self-love forever until the end of time. Thank you for reading my journey, my thoughts, and my perspective. If this book helps you at all or may benefit another, please share it. I am nothing without the people's help. I cannot help people without you, and I am forever indebted to you. Thank you for reading my journal that I call *The Dear Queen Journey: A Path to Self-Love*.

REMEMBER THAT EVERY

BREAKDOWN YOU HAVE IS A

STAIRWAY TO BREAKTHROUGH.

DON'T WORRY TOO HARD YOU

GOT THIS.

Never lose sight of yourself,
Self-awareness and self love
Are two important factors
To happiness.

Final Message To You:

Nobody can save you, nobody can validate you and nobody can tell your story. Your journal is special, your story is special and everything will be okay.

Remember, it is okay not to be "okay", it is okay to show emotion, to be you and to grow as you. Just live, never fear trying something new and most importantly treat yourself better day by day. Loving yourself is more important than any other action.

Accept yourself, love yourself and heal. We gain freedom by releasing the pain and appreciating what we have. Everything will be okay. Love is the most important part of life, seek to understand and grow with it. Seek to give it, seek to be it. Keep your heart, mind and soul open to be love every day of your life. Nothing else truly matters; you are the love of your life. You are the most important person on this planet.

The End

Message from Sylvester:

I'm grateful that you read my journey journal; my only goal is to help people live healthier and happier lives. If I earned you as a friend and reader, please tell your other friends about my art and me. I am a humble man who is foolish enough to believe that I can change the world through sharing my story of struggle. I found self-love after depression and heartbreak. I believe in the power of the universe and the law of attraction. I hope this book brings you closer to self-love, and now, I hope it brings me closer to my queen. If my future queen read this book, just know that we will connect.

Xoxo - Sylvester

Made in the
USA
Lexington, KY